RAPTURE

JOANNA MURRAY-SMITH

CURRENCY PRESS
The performing arts publisher

CURRENCY PLAYS

First published in 2002
by Currency Press Pty Ltd,
PO Box 2287, Strawberry Hills, NSW, 2012, Australia
enquiries@currency.com.au
www.currency.com.au

Copyright © Joanna Murray-Smith, 2002.

Reprinted 2023.

COPYING FOR EDUCATIONAL PURPOSES
The Australian *Copyright Act 1968* (Act) allows a maximum of one chapter or 10% of this book, whichever is the greater, to be copied by any educational institution for its educational purposes provided that that educational institution (or the body that administers it) has given a remuneration notice to Copyright Agency (CA) under the Act.

For details of the CA licence for educational institutions contact CA, 12/66 Goulburn Street, Sydney, NSW, 2000 tel: within Australia 1800 066 844 toll free; outside Australia 61 2 9394 7600; fax: 61 2 9394 7601; email: memberservices@copyright.com.au

COPYING FOR OTHER PURPOSES
Except as permitted under the Act, for example a fair dealing for the purposes of study, research, criticism or review, no part of this book may be reproduced, stored in a retrieval system, or transmitted in any form or by any means without prior written permission. All inquiries should be made to the publisher at the address above.

Any performance or public reading of *Rapture* is forbidden unless a licence has been received from the author or the author's agent. The purchase of this book in no way gives the purchaser the right to perform the plays in public, whether by means of a staged production or a reading. All applications for public performance should be addressed c/- Currency Press.

Typeset by Dean Nottle.
Printed by Fineline Print + Copy Services, Revesby, NSW.
Cover design by Lisa White.

A catalogue record for this book is available from the National Library of Australia

Contents

Rapture   1

For my friends,
Fiona Moshirian and Annie Went

Rapture was first produced by Playbox Theatre at The C.U.B. Malthouse, Melbourne, on 13 November 2002 with the following cast:

HENNY	Marg Downey
DAN	Paul English
EVE	Natasha Herbert
JANE	Belinda McClory
TOM	Neil Pigot
HARRY	Greg Stone

Director, Jenny Kemp
Designer, Dale Ferguson
Lighting Designer, Rachel Burke
Composer, Elizabth Drake
Stage Manager, Kevin de Zilva

CHARACTERS

All the characters are in their early to mid-forties

    EVE, a luminously beautiful woman
    DAN, an attractive man
    TOM, a physically charismatic and stylish man, husband of EVE
    JANE, an attractive woman, wife of DAN
    HENNY, a simply but elegantly dressed woman
    HARRY, a simply but well-dressed man, husband of HENNY

PROLOGUE

HARRY, *forty-six, in a dinner suit, is standing in the spotlight. He is flushed with pleasure, success, alcohol, pride. He speaks directly to the audience.*

HARRY '... Anything—you want.' And the first guy says: 'Anything?' And the beautiful sexy genie says: 'Listen, listen, I said anything, but you can only ask for it in three words.' And he says: 'Okay. Blow Me Hard!' And so the genie obliges. And then the genie says to the second guy: 'Come on now, honey, your turn. Anything you want, anything! But in three words.' So the second guy says: 'Screw Me Now!' So she obliges and it's ecstasy. And then it's the last guy and he says to the beautiful sexy genie: 'So, as long as it's in three words I can have anything?' And she says: 'Anything.' So he says: 'Okay. All right. *Paint My House...*'

Recorded laughter.

Okay, so, that's a joke, okay. But like many jokes, it has a kernel of truth. A man may like a lot of things, but his home, well, as the saying goes, a quaint cottage with room for improvement on a quarter acre can look like it's got turrets and a moat around it to the man who owns it. We all of us—we're dream-dealers. To most people, a house is the soul of their life, the safe haven of their family, the place, sometimes the only place where they can be themselves. To us here tonight, it is all that and more. I only want to say one thing. I'm proud to be a dream-dealer. And I'm proud and honoured that tonight, I am Real Estate Agent of the Year.

Light down on HARRY. *Lights up on* HENNY, *glamorous, forty, supremely confident, again speaking to the audience.*

HENNY: When people ask me what I deal in, I say I deal in 'The Miracle of Daily Life'. The Miracle. Of. Daily. Life. Think about it. Another word for the miracle of daily life? *Style*. It's a word that's become synonymous with superficiality. Well, you know what? Style is about taking ordinary, simple things and honouring them. Making them shine. Don't be ashamed to be stylish! A meal on kitchen crockery on a plain wooden table becomes something more when we add a posy of simple kitchen garden herbs and flowers, some nicely pressed white damask table napkins, properly shined cutlery and a really, *really* nice family. When we take the time to do it right, we're talking about heightening the experience of life itself. The simple homely meal is worth getting right because it is an offering: an offering of friendship, an offering of love. Every recipe you see tonight is available in my new book, *A Jug of Wine, a Loaf of Bread and Thou*, available in all good book stores at a recommended retail price of $39.95. Remember. Five little letters, but the foundation of a life worth living. Style. What else is there?

SCENE ONE

An Autumn evening. A smart, sophisticated, slightly arty, modern living/ dining room, equipped with a drinks tray (from which the characters help themselves and each other through the course of the play).

EVE, *unselfconsciously beautiful and stylish, forty-ish, is surveying an elegant dinner table set for six, to which she is putting the finishing touches.* DAN, *handsome but not especially stylish, early forties, enters with a smart shopping bag. He studies* EVE *with a particular kind of intensity for a long moment, enjoying the sight of her, before speaking.*

DAN: Ugly sisters leave you at home then?
EVE: [*without looking up, but smiling*] Still peddling that old line?
DAN: It used to work. [*Beat.*] So they're coming.
EVE: [*contemplating the setting of cutlery*] Apparently. [*Beat.*] What do you think about dessert spoons?
DAN: I'm very fond of them and I'm not afraid to say it.
EVE: What about the 'side or above' rule?
DAN: Above Board or On the Side? You know me.
EVE: Equivocal?
DAN: I take my dessert any way it comes. [*Beat. Taking a seat*] So they're actually coming.

EVE *fixes herself and* DAN *a drink.*

EVE: Apparently they are. Apparently they are coming.
DAN: Well, what's going on? When did they get back?
EVE: I don't know. No one knows anything.
DAN: But they're definitely coming?
EVE: Apparently, they're coming.

> EVE *passes* DAN *his drink. They raise their glasses, silently, to one another.* EVE *sits.*

DAN: Where's Tom?
EVE: I sent him out for Bolivian capers.
DAN: All my life I've dreamt about a woman who would actually *urge* me to have adventures in South America.
EVE: The *other* capers.
DAN: And The Oracle?
EVE: At my mother's. It's been mad around here—Tom's been hounded by journalists. It was better for her—well, you know—
DAN: Sure—
EVE: Eddie's still away—?
DAN: The school says he's learning life skills. You know, for all the wood-chopping and orienteering he'll be doing as a D.J. at raves. Where's the nanny?
EVE: You remember the one with fish-nets?
DAN: Who could forget?
EVE: Vanished. The Oracle was too much for her.
DAN: Still wandering off?
EVE: Still doing things—
DAN: Yes—
EVE: You know. *Things.*

> *They look at each other. There's history there.*

We saw the American.
DAN: And—?
EVE: The same as all the others. Somehow, being American, I thought perhaps—
DAN: Yes—
EVE: Something to do with the teeth—
DAN: Exactly!
EVE: But he said it was all about a drum.
DAN: A drum?

EVE: Apparently she marches to the beat of a different one.
DAN: That was it?
EVE: It's good to know that's what a specialist gets you. The most apposite use of a cliche.
DAN: She's bright—
EVE: She's *eerily* bright—which is not something one should encourage.
DAN: Did you give some thought—?
EVE: I did. Honestly, I did, Dan. But I don't think she's ready—
DAN: I'm not thinking of her. [*Beat.*] They want you back.
EVE: Then *I'm* not ready. You know, a mother's love is not *despite* a child's difficulty, it's *because* of it.
DAN: [*breaking the moment*] Before I forget—I brought her something. [*Taking it from his pocket*] It's probably a little old-fashioned for a kid these days.
EVE: A compass?
DAN: This was mine. My father gave it to me. I was going to give it to Eddie, but you know. He's only interested in things that plug in.
EVE: [*taking it*] You're sweet to her. Thank you.
DAN: Tell her Uncle Dan said he missed her.
EVE: She doesn't call you 'Uncle Dan'. She calls you 'Blazey'. A ten-year-old with the infuriating habit of calling me 'Wife' and Tom 'Husband'. She calls out: 'Wife! Where's my Paddle Pop?'
DAN: Charming.
EVE: Tom says that all she really wants is Psycho-Barbie, who rips the arms off Ken and boils her pet bunny.
DAN: I'll be sure and get her one for Christmas.

A moment as DAN *acknowledges* EVE*'s carefully camouflaged sorrow.* DAN *takes a shoe box out of the shopping bag.*

And this is for you.
EVE: You brought me—?

She opens the box and takes a very beautiful, elegant shoe from the tissue.

Shoes.
DAN: Yes.
EVE: *You brought me a pair of shoes?*
DAN: Yes.
EVE: [*taken aback*] Well. Well. They're lovely.

DAN: [*certain*] You like shoes.
EVE: I *do* like shoes.
DAN: They're your size.
EVE: They are my size. They certainly *are* my size.
DAN: You like them?
EVE: [*she loves them*] I like them *a lot*.
DAN: [*a moment of doubt*] But you have enough shoes?
EVE: You can never have—
DAN: That's what I thought—
EVE: *Never*.

She takes off her shoes and puts them in the box and puts on the new ones, which look beautiful, fit perfectly, match her outfit.

DAN: Is it wrong?
EVE: It *seems* wrong.
DAN: It *does* seem wrong.

They both stare at her feet in silence for a few moments.

EVE: Where's Jane?
DAN: Another funding application.
EVE: Forgive me. But if Jane is ever given funding, I'm demanding a refund from the tax department.
DAN: I'll pretend I didn't hear that. Table looks perfect.

She turns back to the table and surveys it critically.

EVE: It's deeply symbolic—the dining table. Yourself down one end, your husband down the other, the twin pillars of a chosen life—the country of marriage spread out between you—
DAN: Between you, the population of a marriage…
EVE: The friend you meant to love but somehow couldn't, the friends you define yourself against, those you wish you might change and those you wish might change you, the moralist, the hedonist, the joker and over the course of the evening, an unruly government topples and settles, gaining principles, jettisoning policies, one moment all in agreement, the next divided—and there it is. There it is, the drunks and the cynics and the angels, drinking and laughing and weeping, a few hours, a few decades, a life.
DAN: We were young for so long and then all of a sudden, we were old.
EVE: I was just thinking… You know, I lust after my earlier self—
DAN: That makes two of us—

EVE: Skinny. Those breasts that seemed to live independent lives.
DAN: Independent breasts. That's nostalgia for you.
EVE: Everything ahead and somehow... glowing. Glowing with... it wasn't innocence, was it? It was simply the thought that anything was possible.
DAN: *Isn't* anything possible?
EVE: No. No. And partly because the things one once thought of as attractive possibilities aren't that attractive anymore. I mean, I don't *want* to drive to Phoenix with the son of a Princeton professor. I don't *want* to swim naked in the moonlight... very often.
DAN: What a relief to banish the allure of youth—
EVE: Every aspect of character was forced to explain itself. Socialism. Buddhism. Environmentalism. [*Beat.*] Now I'm perfectly certain there is no ideology on Earth more gripping than fashion.
DAN: *Are* there Bolivian capers?
EVE: No.
DAN: I didn't think so.
EVE: Whenever we have people for dinner, he starts talking *at* me. As if I'm his warm-up routine.
DAN: So you send him out on an impossible errand.
EVE: Whipped Madagascan lychees or cryovacked yeast.
DAN: Yeast not being commonly cryovacked.
EVE: Oh, Tom thinks it *comes* from Cryovac.

   They smile.

I suppose the tragedy was I didn't really know that one might lose things by not acquiring them. I thought things could be... put off until I'd learned, finally, if I wanted them or not. And then, when finally I looked around... they were gone.
DAN: You had a 'thing' for artists.
EVE: I did. That arrogance—an artist's arrogance, that which makes them—convinced by themselves. [*Beat.*] For the longest time I lived as if other lives would one day be available— Somehow with The Oracle, those days and weeks after I had her, I got it. That with every choice, a million possibilities vanish forever. It seems disingenuous to say it—but once a mother, that sensation of aloneness is never again available. Some people must have children to escape aloneness—but I—I long for it...

DAN: [*very carefully*] Eve, you need—*she* needs—
EVE: Well, you know—
DAN: Does he *talk* to her—?
EVE: Well, you know, he *talks*—
DAN: Does he actually *talk* to her—?
EVE: [*unconvinced*] She'll be all right. *I'll* be—you know, all right. I just miss unfixed, ordinary attachments instead of this intolerable belonging—this casual insanity of child-having—
DAN: You know I—
EVE: Dan, I'm not sure you can—
DAN: I understand 'unrequited'—
EVE: [*with intensity*] No. Don't— [*Beat. Diffusing*] Strange word, 'requited'. There are some words you rarely hear without the prefix. It sounds so—naked.
DAN: Perhaps the only love worth speaking of is thwarted love. The only love that ends as it began—
EVE: Full strength.

> *They look at each other. A long beat. Sadness.*

DAN: [*with breezy effort*] Actually, one of the great pleasures of getting older has been the acknowledgment that I despise artists.
EVE: You do?
DAN: I used to pretend to believe in them, as some insecure confirmation that I was a cultivated sort of person, you know, as if a fondness for a woman who slathers herself in chocolate sauce then wraps herself in barbed wire as some kind of lyrical comment on the holocaust, would define me as *not* a philistine. But I've come to the conclusion that art, by and large, *is* vulgarity. While people are starving and locked in detention centres and children are blown up by suicide bombers…
EVE: Tom will be thrilled to hear it.
DAN: Tom *counts* on my disapproval. [*Casual, jaunty*] How is it, by the way?
EVE: How is—?
DAN: Your marriage.
EVE: [*the hint of sadness*] I suppose it's… what it ought to be. Two people deciding whether the new door handles should be chrome or matt. 'Chrome is sharper', says he. 'Matt is subtler', says I. 'Tim

and Alison have matt', says he. 'Then so must we', says I, 'since we must all have the same. Everyone of us. In our houses. We must all have the same or What Might Happen?' That sort of thing can go on for a couple of years before you need a new topic to carry you through dinner. Oh, and I love him.

DAN: Love, is it?

EVE: [*playful but not remotely convincing*] Well, you know, he's got awfully important lately and importance is, disgustingly, a major aphrodisiac.

DAN: I always wanted to be important but I decided, in the end, it was more important to work on my thighs.

EVE: You're a little bit important.

DAN: Only you could get away with a compliment like that. Listen, there's the one who writes about and the one who is written about. We can't all be the stars.

EVE: No, some of us have to be the starfuckers. No starfuckers, no stars.

DAN: I interviewed Talbot Jones today.

EVE: Lucky you.

DAN: He wasn't all that bright. And I know you like bright men.

EVE: When I was still at the company, I tried very hard to sign him—

DAN: 'Sign' being a publisher's code-word for—

EVE: You're being very impertinent. I never slept with any of my writers—

DAN: Until Tom—

EVE: Well, I *was* married to him, so I felt it was probably appropriate to make an exception. But Tom not withstanding, I always felt Talbot Jones was one of those rare writers you'd like to sit next to at a dinner party.

DAN: Let me dispel that little myth. He has a mid-life earring.

EVE: No!

DAN: Yes!

EVE: Not a mid-life earring!

DAN: Yes! Yes! Terrible but true!

They smile.

EVE: [*changing the mood, as if she has to confess*] After we saw the American—we were in the parking lot of the Children's Hospital. We were getting in the car—Tom and me in front—The Oracle in the back—and she said— [*Beat.*] She said: 'It's too late—'

DAN: It's too—?

EVE: Late.
DAN: It's too late?
EVE: Yes. To go back.

They look at each other.

It's too late to go back. [*Beat.*] She said it. [*Beat.*] I'm half expecting the phone call that announces catastrophe. You know how it goes— an ordinary sentence, a little joke interrupted by the ring, at first innocent, then growing more sinister at each insistent bell—and the knowledge that this pause between hearing and answering may very well be the divide between what was once and some brutal future. All this fuss about paedophiles on every street corner, when what every mother fears the most is in nearly every room of every house of every street. These little boxes. These mad little boxes full of stories they can't wait to spill. Mayhem. Disaster. Misery. Is there anything more terrifying than the sound of a telephone?

He moves towards her, touches her hand—

DAN: Eve.

Beat. She studies him.

EVE: You look tired.
DAN: I *am* tired.
EVE: What are you tired of?
DAN: Missing things.

A glance of longing between them. TOM *enters, bringing a wave of energy effortlessly with him.* DAN *stands and the two men hug.* DAN *pours* TOM *a drink as* TOM *sinks into a chair.*

TOM: [*up, up, up*] Lovely article this week!
DAN: [*fully expecting this*] Thanks.
TOM: You think of that, did you? 'Ten ways to improve your day'?

DAN *passes* TOM *the drink.*

DAN: Actually, I did.
TOM: I especially loved the one about walking on a deserted beach.
DAN: I'm so glad.
TOM: I was somewhat surprised, however, that you didn't include playing with a puppy in the sunshine.
DAN: I had to leave something for next time.
TOM: That explains it! So what do you think? They're coming.

DAN: So it seems—
TOM: God knows, it wasn't easy—
DAN: When did they get back?
TOM: No one knows. I suppose they'll tell us tonight—we might actually get some answers—
DAN: Are they all right?
TOM: Who knows? I went ahead and booked the house for summer. They're just going to have to go with the dates. Every man and his dog is after a rental.
EVE: Capers?
TOM: A calamity. The ignorance of some people is astonishing. The delicatessen manager had never even heard of Bolivian capers! I said: 'Good God, woman, you're trying to run an inner-city delicatessen without Bolivian capers? Are you disorganised or Just Plain Mad?'

He puts a small jar down in front of EVE *with a thud.*

Warragul capers. [*Beat. Without the slightest hint of concern*] You two look cosy.
EVE: We *are* cosy.
DAN: I suppose you're feeling pretty pleased with yourself?
TOM: No more than usual.
DAN: Yes, well that would be superfluous.
TOM: Should I try to be less successful, do you think?
DAN: You may not have to try as hard as you think. [*Raising his glass and with affection*] Congratulations Tom. I'm very happy for you. It's a real honour.
TOM: [*flatly*] It's nothing really. Prizes are meaningless. The book is no better or worse than before it won.
DAN: [*not buying it for a second*] One more time, with conviction.
TOM: [*equally flatly*] It's nothing really. Prizes are meaningless. The book is no better or worse than before it won.

They smile.

DAN: [*looking at his prize*] Do awards *have* to be hideous, do you think? Would one feel cheated with a prize that was attractive?
EVE: *The Times* called it 'a comic masterpiece'. They said it 'captured the obnoxiously effervescent self-congratulation of the late baby-boomers'. They doubled the print run.
DAN: The protagonist, Fitzgerald, the documentary film-maker—

TOM: Well, I hope I pulled it off: sardonic but not superior. I must say, at the risk of sounding slightly oversatisfied—middle age is actually rather good.
EVE: At the risk. At the slight risk.
TOM: Freed from all the dithering, skinny panic of youth, all that wishfulness, all that fear of amounting to zero, all those 'How did you get theres?' and no end to the rainforests one felt personally responsible for. Freed from all that, and prior to the nursing home and little pieces of sponge cut into exact squares on fat, white china. Sandwiched in there a chapter of knowing what it is one amounts to and, if it's allowed, an occasional acknowledgment that the zero is banished, is overcome. One *is* something. One *has* a beautiful wife. One has managed to find something, something linen-y, something muted, wavering between taste and judgement.
EVE: Well, that's all very well, Tom, but did you know, Talbot Jones has a mid-life earring?
TOM: No!
EVE & DAN: [*together*] Yes!
TOM: What? A little ring or a diamond stud.
DAN: Stud. A la Harrison Ford. Who once played the President of the United States and now looks like he sells 'armoires'.
TOM: You weren't interviewing that prat, were you?
DAN: I know. It's ridiculous to even contemplate any other writer deserves attention.
TOM: 'The anodyne expression of the man reminded Prescott of the spurious agony of a lost child.' I mean, with prose like that, no *wonder* he got an earring. He needs every distracting appendage available.
DAN: You actually memorised that?
TOM: It was no effort, believe me. It's the perfect warning bell to keep on tap to remind one of the pitfalls of rampant creativity.

JANE, early forties, attractive, fashionable but somehow missing elegance, enters.

JANE: [*on a wave of completely-in-the-moment fury*] MOTHERFUCKERS! [*Beat. At rapid speed*] Those motherfuckers in their motherfucking suits! Those big fat motherfuckers in their Hugo Boss sitting on their fat butts in their boxer shorts with their pay cheques that come in every week thinking about the big fat beef ribs and mashed potato they're going to eat for dinner with a big fat fruity fucking shiraz and all the people they're going to fuck over tomorrow and all the people, all the dreamers, all the thinkers, all the darers, all the adventurers they're going to stymie and squash and humiliate and destroy and how good it makes them feel, how big and clever and rich and successful and immortal and *sexy* it makes them feel because they're scared of ideas and they're scared of what they don't understand and because they think art has to be what art has been before or it's not art and because they think artists have to look and speak and move a certain way to be artists otherwise they can't be sure they really *are* artists and once they realise they don't really know about that they realise they don't really know about anything and if they don't really know about anything they might be obsolete and if they're obsolete they can't afford their fruity fucking shirazes!

Beat.

DAN: No funding?

JANE: [*completely deflated*] No funding.

EVE *and* TOM *catch each other's eye.* EVE *passes* JANE *the drink she's been pouring, which* JANE *takes without acknowledging.*

DAN: What did they say?

JANE: They said that 'while it was clearly an interesting concept with significant sociological comment, it didn't meet their current criteria for imaginative vision'.

EVE: Bad luck, darling.

JANE: I mean, for God's sake! How much *more* relevant could a project be?

TOM: This is the documentary about the siblings of famous people?

JANE: Yes. Deidre Rush, Geoffrey's sister—an accountant. Darren Spielberg—Kosher caterer. Cyril Streep… We've got everyone! Of course they didn't get the title—

DAN: I warned you—

JANE: —*Brother, Can You Spare a Dime?* They said: 'What does that mean?' I said: 'The resentment of being outside celebrity: the insecurities, the sense of being cheated by destiny.' Right over their heads. [*Beat.*] I explained—*well*, I think—that it was a symbolic examination of the fundamental importance of the notion of equality—as a central tenet of Western civilisation.

TOM: Oh Jane! Equality's drastically overrated. I *like* the fact that there are fat cats smoking cigars in penthouses while low-lifes clean

windscreens at intersections beneath them…
DAN: There's one cliche you forgot: the pompous writer with his glass of sauvignon blanc pontificating in the inner city—
TOM: [*undeterred*] Hate, envy, malice… these are the things that make life interesting. Imagine how boring it would be if everyone drove a station wagon and lived in the suburbs, going from barbecue to fundraiser with a bunch of kids covered in sunblock, suspended in mediocrity, stringing fairy lights around their unexceptional lives—
JANE: He gets tremendous pleasure from inciting violence.
TOM: Life's unfair and that's a good thing. Without injustice there would be no art, or marriage or even friendship—since they are all either the expression of injustice or the refuge from it.
EVE: You're showing off appallingly again, darling.
TOM: But, darling, you love me this way.
EVE: [*to* JANE, *with just a hint of surprise*] Is that what you wore?
JANE: [*confused, alarmed*] This?
EVE: No, I mean it's fine—
JANE: Is it the colours—?
EVE: [*unconvincing but not unkind*] You get away with it.
JANE: I really thought this was going to be the year—
TOM: [*it's an old argument*] Jane, do we *care* about celebrity siblings?
JANE: Yes, Tom! Yes. I mean, people like you are the reason that this film *must* be made! Anyway, They're coming?
TOM: Yes. Yes, they're coming.
JANE: Do we know—?
DAN: We know—
JANE: They're definitely—?
TOM: They're coming. They *are* coming.

    JANE *raises her glass, slightly stiffly, to* TOM.

JANE: [*slightly coolly*] Congratulations, Tom. We were thrilled.
TOM: Thank you, my love, but really it's nothing. Prizes are meaningless. The book is no better or worse than before it won.
DAN: Still not quite *landing*, if you know what I mean.
JANE: [*still slightly cool*] *The Times* called it 'brilliant'. You can't do better than that.
TOM: [*playfully petulant*] Talbot Jones's book was 'important'.
DAN: 'Important' is five stars. 'Brilliant' three and a half. One and a half stars can be your personal Everest.

TOM: Your time will come. In the meantime, here's a great idea for a column: Your best friend wins a big prize— It could be a hilarious sulk about why *him* sort of thing when it should have been *me*. How's the car by the way?
DAN: Terrific.
TOM: Running well?
DAN: Purring like a pussy cat.
TOM: I'm pleased.
JANE: Where's The Oracle?
EVE: At my mother's.
JANE: How is she?
TOM: Well, she hasn't been found in a neighbouring state this week, so we're feeling rather high.
JANE: The nanny's gone?
TOM: Without trace. We suspect The Oracle murdered her.
EVE: Tom!
TOM: She's up there in the toy box, all chopped up into little pieces. The only tell-tale sign: an empty pair of fish-nets.
They laugh. TOM *suddenly notices* EVE's *feet.*
New shoes?
EVE: *Very* new.
JANE: Anyway, shouldn't they be here?
DAN: We should have said, seven— With them you have to allow—
EVE: They'll be here. If they said they would—
TOM: Actually, I'm glad they're late. Gives us a chance to—well—gather ourselves.
DAN: When did you hear they were back?
JANE: Caroline Tanner. Told Sandra and Robbie. Robbie told Tom at Ben Tavistock's book launch.
TOM: Caroline had actually glimpsed Henny—
DAN: Where?
EVE: In the lobby of the Hyatt.
TOM: Caroline was meeting some CEO from out of town for a breakfast meeting—
EVE: And she virtually jumped out of her skin—
TOM: Henny in the distance talking to the reservations people. By the time Caroline stood up—
EVE: She was gone.

TOM: Caroline called Paul pronto.
DAN: Who's Paul Pronto?
TOM: Paul, you idiot! She called Paul, who happened to be playing squash with Robbie and as soon as he arrived at the club for the launch, he told me.
EVE: Obviously they were back.
TOM: I practically dropped my mini-bruschetta. I found a quiet corner and called the Hyatt and asked to be put through to Harry Denton and before you knew it, Harry was on the actual line.
EVE: Tell them about—
TOM: Well—
EVE: What *you* said. What *they* said.
JANE: Did they know we'd been trying—? *No one* knew their itinerary.
DAN: We'd tried—
EVE: I know—
JANE: Henny's mother told me she 'wasn't at liberty'— I mean, for God's sake! We're only their best friends! But what was I going to do? Get an eighty-two-year-old in a headlock?
DAN: Terry and Meg tried *lots* of times. The Pritchards tried. How many times did you—?
EVE: *Many*—
TOM: So—
JANE: Go on—
TOM: I just decided to tackle it straight on— I said—
EVE: This was great—
TOM: I said: 'What is going on?' Harry. I mean: 'What is going on, Harry?' I said: 'You know we've been *trying*—'
JANE: Good—
TOM: 'We haven't— It's been nearly a year. We tried to find you. And now you're back and we find out third-hand— Dan and Jane—'
DAN: You told him?
TOM: Yes. 'Dan and Jane have— We've all tried— God knows—'
JANE: And—?
TOM: I said: 'We're hurt, Harry'. I said: 'This is hurtful to us'. I said: 'We're your friends'.
DAN: And?
TOM: Nothing. Silence. The longest time.
EVE: So—

TOM: I said: 'Come for dinner. Sunday. Like it used to be. Just the six of us.'
EVE: Wait for this.
TOM: He said: 'I'm not sure we can do that, Tom'. Well, that was just— I mean, come on! I said: 'Harry, you're coming for dinner! I don't care what else you've got on, you're cancelling. I mean, for Christ's sake!' Then he passed the phone to Henny—as if—well—
EVE: He was too scared—
TOM: And she said: 'Okay, Tom. We'll come.' Like she'd— As if she'd been listening on the extension. I said: 'Henny? How are you, Henny?' And there was a—
EVE: This is weird—
TOM: A pause. And she said: 'We're All Right, Tom'—
EVE: Not 'Alright,' but 'All Right'. There's a—
JANE: Yes—
EVE: Difference. 'We're All Right, Tom.' Now doesn't that suggest to you—
DAN: Exactly—
EVE: That they're *not*—
JANE: No—
EVE: *Not* all right. They're *not* all right.

Beat.

JANE: How long—?
EVE: Has it—?
JANE: Yes. How long has it been?
TOM: Seven months. And perhaps I'm wrong— But I think it's enough. I think they've been out there—
JANE: Out there in—
TOM: Doing what one does—whatever it is one does— They've been grieving perhaps—or—or—dealing with it—for seven months and it's my belief they now need—hauling in. They need to be thrown a line—
JANE: Is that what we're doing?
TOM: I think so. Yes. Throwing them the line of friendship—or—or—
DAN: Continuity—
TOM: Hauling them back to the real—
EVE: World. The real world—
TOM: Whatever *that* is— But whatever it is, it's this.

Beat.

EVE: How often does—? I mean— Catastrophe— We don't call—
JANE: No—
EVE: If we were poor. If we were hungry. But we're never hungry—
TOM: I'm hungry. I'm looking forward to some Warragul capers.
EVE: We offer friendship too lightly, too easily, because we know how unlikely it is that our friends will ask anything of us—
DAN: That's exactly right.
EVE: How often do we say to each other: 'I need rescuing?' How far would we go?
JANE: How far would we—?
EVE: We need to ask ourselves— Because I don't know—
TOM: We know that—
EVE: Do we? Do we know that?—
TOM: Dan and Jane and Henny and Harry—they're—well— It doesn't have to be said—
EVE: Then everything important stays silent—

Beat.

DAN: Perhaps— Well, yes. Perhaps things stay—underground— We protect ourselves from—
JANE: From?
DAN: You know, we grow up and we look around and we say: 'I had better make myself appear to have a life. I'd better get what's necessary.' We start collecting. We collect degrees and diplomas. We collect people. We collect quirks—you know, like funny cufflinks, like parking badly—the things people can use when they have to make a birthday speech about you— We collect that stuff so that when we wake up in the morning we don't have to ask why or what for. The props stop us from the terror of that. That's the job of friendship—but—
TOM: I feel an earring coming on.
JANE: You think too much. You all think far too much. If only you could just turn it off.
DAN: [*picking up her cue for lightness, air, change of mood*] She's always wanted me to be able to *do* stuff. I told her when I married her: I can't do stuff. If that's the kind of person you want, don't marry me, but she married me anyway. And doomed me to a lifetime of sexual fantasies where I have to be a carpenter.
JANE: Dan!

DAN: Hand me the lathe, I say. Just planing this piece of hardwood and she's off and running—
JANE: Very funny.
DAN: Which would be all very well except that in my fantasies I'm *not* a carpenter.
I've got nothing against carpenters, I just don't *relate* to them.
EVE: So what would you be? In your fantasies, I mean?
DAN: Oh, a— [*Suddenly losing confidence*] A— [*Beat. Then realising he might as well say it*] A shepherd.
TOM, JANE & EVE: [*together, laughing*] What!
DAN: I think shepherds are very sexy. Very.
EVE: *I* don't mind a carpenter—
JANE: Where do you meet them though? I mean, are there carpenters' bars?
EVE: Across the nation, women married to dentists and writers and postal clerks are asking that very question.
JANE: They'd be very nice bars, wouldn't they? I mean, nice wood, well turned.
TOM: All right. Enough.
JANE: The thing about carpenters is, they're both lyrical *and* jaunty.

Their laughter is interrupted by the doorbell. They all turn towards the door. Blackout.

SCENE TWO

Lights up on TOM, EVE, DAN, JANE *gathered around* HARRY *and* HENNY, *who are sitting stiffly, formally, next to each other on the sofa.* HENNY *and* HARRY *are in their mid-forties, neatly but simply dressed. Everyone has a drink, it's clear the greetings are long done with.* HENNY *and* HARRY *have a tone of unvarying neutrality, a matter of factness in the way they speak. There's an intensity, quietness to the way the others listen to them, as if they are witnessing a spell.*

HENNY: We stopped at Burger King. [*Beat.*] That night. We stopped at Burger King. On the way home. Harry wanted a cheeseburger. The catering had been dreadful.

18

HARRY: We were hungry.
HENNY: We unwrapped— Well, we ate on the way. I said to Harry, it's just as well someone thought of beverage holders because they make life so much simpler. We were driving slowly and it was dark. The road was icy. A couple of times we skidded a little bit and I told Harry not to hurry. The next day was Sunday. We didn't need to be anywhere. I thought I might plan a dinner for—well, for all of us, maybe ask someone new too—maybe Tess and William McBain from the paper—she's interesting—I wanted to try some new recipes, a scallop dish and a poppy-seed cake with lime syrup. I thought I'd try them out on the Sunday—have a domestic day. There was a fox on the road when we took the bend near the Bedford turn-off and Harry braked and swerved and, before you knew it, we were on the wrong side of the road, inches from a big old elm tree. Harry and I—well—neither of us said anything for a minute. We just sat there, staring at the trunk of the tree and fog illuminated by the headlights and then I felt this sensation, this well, *levity* and I said: 'Imagine if they found the author of *The Glamorous Gourmet* sprawled dead in her car and strewn with Burger King wrappers?' And we laughed. The two of us in our big fancy car thinking we were somebodies, thinking we were somebodies with our books and our house and our espresso maker and our famous artist etchings—dead and bleeding and covered in styrofoam containers. Then Harry started the car. We pulled back out on the road and I put my hand on Harry's knee and I said to him: 'In all the years we've been together, I've never been bored by you. But if I died just then—if something happened to us—Something Big—I could not say that I understood the point.' And Harry kept driving and then he said: 'Well, perhaps it's just a matter of *making* a point. Of *making* a point or *finding* one. Maybe points aren't there as a matter of course.' And then we took a right off the main road and we were moving along Bakers Road and we passed the Martins' and the Thomas's barn and that's when we saw the glow… [*Beat.*] The glowing.

    Long beat.

JANE: Henny—
HENNY: It's all right. Really. It's—well—
JANE: It must have been dreadful—

HENNY: Well… Well…
JANE: We've been—we've wanted to help—to help—but—
HENNY: I know—
EVE: You never answered. I mean—we kept trying but—
JANE: No one had your itinerary. We wanted to write—
HENNY: Yes.
TOM: We wanted *you* to know—
EVE: We were worried. We wanted to help.
HENNY: We weren't ready, Eve. That's all I can say.
EVE: When did you get back?
HARRY: [*sheepish*] Well…
EVE: Where were you?
HENNY: [*awkwardly*] We didn't really— We didn't really travel.
JANE: But were you in London? Or Paris?
HENNY: No.
DAN: We thought you might be in Tuscany. We thought you might have gone back to that place near Luca—
HENNY: We contemplated Luca.
EVE: So—?
HARRY: We were at the Hyatt.

Beat.

EVE: No, but I mean, where were you overseas?
HENNY: We weren't actually overseas.

Beat. They are all disconcerted.

DAN: Where were you?
HENNY: We were here.
EVE: Here?
HENNY: Yes. We never left.
JANE: What?
HARRY: We were at the Hyatt. I mean, that's where we were.
DAN: But we never— For seven months you've been at the Hyatt?
HARRY: That's right.
JANE: *You've been at the Hyatt?*
HARRY: We had a suite. Insurance paid.
DAN: *At the Hyatt?*
HARRY: *Big* suite. Couple of bathrooms. Three TVs!
TOM: *For seven months?*

20

HARRY: [*minimising, lightly*] Actually, you get pretty used to it.
EVE: You never went to Europe?
HENNY: No. No. I mean, we really didn't leave the Hyatt.
JANE: But we haven't seen you.
DAN: I mean, no one's bumped into you—at the, you know—*about*—
HARRY: Well, that's because we just haven't been out at all.
DAN: Yes, but—you know—just *around*—
HARRY: No. No. This is the first time—
HENNY: Tonight.
TOM: You're telling us that this is the first time you've walked out the door of the Hyatt?
HENNY: Yes. Yes, it is.
DAN: *For seven months?*
HENNY: Yes. But you know, there are really not very many reasons to leave.
HARRY: Three TVs!
EVE: There aren't many reasons to leave the hotel? For seven months?
HENNY: No. I mean, it has a doctor. There's a hairdresser and a health spa. The chefs are actually quite good and if you're there for a while, they'll make you pretty much anything you want.
HARRY: A really *excellent* Caesar Salad—
HENNY: Became a bit of a staple!
HARRY: There's cable. There are movies. There's a library. The internet. Travis—that's the concierge—Travis will get you any stuff you might—you know, socks or—or—whatever. I mean, think about it. What country on Earth supplies you with a robe at the border?
TOM: *What?*
HARRY: It's actually a nice kind of a place. It's clean. There are fountains in the foyer that are— I liked the fountains. There are people coming through. People you wouldn't seek out, exactly, but since they're there, they're actually not bad people. You get to chatting in the elevator. Broadens your horizons.
TOM: You spent seven months at the Hyatt talking to people in the elevator? While we thought you were picking porcini mushrooms in Umbria, you were actually on the corner of Russell and Collins?
HENNY: We contemplated Luca. But we were at the Hyatt.

Beat. The others look at each other subtly indicating their shock. For the moment, they want to preserve politeness.

JANE: We felt— We felt— Well, Gosh, Henny. We felt terrible.
HENNY: Thank you.
DAN: That's why we were so frustrated. I mean, our best friends have just experienced... this terrible blow and then... vanished.
HARRY: It must have seemed that way.
JANE: We were desolate. We wanted to take you in... comfort you—
DAN: We had ideas. About you staying with— About putting together a new library for you—
HENNY: We appreciate that. Really, we do.
HARRY: We do appreciate that.
HENNY: But, you see, it's not that we felt so bad—that's the thing—we actually felt— Harry—?
HARRY: As it happens—it was—
HENNY: Yes—
HARRY: It was a good—
HENNY: Yes—
EVE: It was a good—?
HARRY: Thing. Yes.
HENNY: [*neutral, calm, poised*] That's right. It was the best thing that ever happened to us.

Beat.

DAN: Your house burning down?
HENNY: We weren't aware of that in the moment. In the moment it was a shock. We got out of the car and we stood there and we watched the flames.
HARRY: Later—later we went through...
HENNY: The inventory of significant losses. That's what we called it. The photograph albums. My mother's wedding dress. The maps. The Matisse lithograph. The books—my bound sets of Austen and Eliot and Dickens, Pepys, the first editions of Patrick White... My manuscripts, recipes... The journals I kept for twenty years tracking the detail of a life, showing the junctions and intersections, the places where destiny collided with choice— The letters Harry had written me in the early days, two parts naivete to one part lust, full of hope, full of some doubtful tenderness impossible now to resurrect, scraps of paper with messages written in haste that I had kept as mementos of casual love... All of it, tiny flickers in the flames...

HARRY: We went— First of all we just went to the Holiday Inn. Since that was closest. Someone drove us there. I can't even remember now. Henny made tea and we got into bed, those cheap hotel sheets, and we held each other and it was then that it first occurred to me... Well, I remember thinking: it's still burning. Smouldering, to be exact—since the firemen had put out the flames. But inside the ashes there were still embers glowing, feeding from the stuff of our life, chewing it up. And I started to think about fire. How alive it is. How 'active' it is. And there seemed to me something quite... beautiful in that.
TOM: [*softly, wondering*] Harry?
HARRY: All the artefacts of a life being lit—lit up—and reforming into—the glowing. The glowing. What was inside the glowing if not something good?
HENNY: And in the morning, we got up and showered and got dressed and had our breakfast and we sort of just looked at each other and said: 'Well, what do we do?'
HARRY: 'What do we do?'
HENNY: What do you do when everything is gone but your body and your lover? Your body and your lover and your memory and—the wish to do something good and purposeful? You don't quite realise that when you don't have a house, you don't really have anywhere to 'be'. And we started laughing. Harry and me, laughing on the doorstep of room nineteen at the Holiday Inn, in our fancy clothes from the night before, blue velvet dress, Harry in a tux! Drinking Nescafe and *absolutely no place to go*.
HARRY: And from that moment on, it was—we were— Something just... well...
TOM: What?
HARRY: Well, it's kind of hard to explain.
TOM: Well, well, *try*—
HARRY: I don't know that you're going to understand, Tom.
TOM: What wouldn't I understand? How long have we been friends, Harry? Thirty, nearly forty years.
HARRY: Well, yes—
TOM: So—?
HARRY: Something was— It's hard to put into words—
TOM: I insist—I insist you try.

23

HARRY: Well—
HENNY: It was as if—
TOM: Go on—
HARRY: Something was… waking up inside of us— Something—
HENNY: New—
HARRY: Yes—
DAN: You'd been through something big. That can… rearrange your priorities.
EVE: You probably had a million things going on—
HENNY: A new—not thought, not idea—no.
JANE: Well—
HARRY: This might seem a little 'general' to you—
DAN: Go on—
JANE: We're—
HARRY: Well, all right, then—perhaps it was not so much the *getting* of something as… [*beat*] … the *release* of something. As if something had—
HENNY: Just vanished. There we were, in our finery, watching the parking lot, the identical doors, the numbers, the car spaces, the breakfast trays on the porches with demolished Cornflakes packets and jam sachets—I thought to myself, each of those rooms tells a story. In each of those rooms there is a fire, a loss, an abandoning, a transition, a regret, a birth—*stories*— And the question has to be asked: What gives us the strength—?
HARRY: That's what we wondered—
HENNY: All of us. In our motel rooms. What gives us the strength to survive the collateral of disappointment?
  Silence.
JANE: Well, well. That's a good question.
DAN: It certainly is. It's a fair question. Having gone through what you've been through.
JANE: We *find* the strength. Somehow. We just—
EVE: [*at them but not to them*] That's right. We live our lives—keeping quiet, holding on—holding on, as if the slightest relaxation will undo us. We must be vigilant. We must notice some, but not too much. We find a way to endure—through openings and closings, the death of friends or their renewals, the soft, disappearing footsteps of love…

Somehow— Somehow—who could believe the strength?
HENNY: The thing is— We found that we had— Well, we went to the Hyatt and after a week or two we started to talk about what we were going to do next.
HARRY: Where we'd go. What we'd do.
HENNY: We actually talked about calling you. Of course we did.
HARRY: But for some reason we found that we—
HENNY: Just couldn't pick up the phone. We'd just— We'd lift the receiver and then we'd put it back again.
HARRY: It wasn't just you. It was pretty much everybody.
HENNY: We'd say: 'Well, today, we really ought to call so and so and so and so'. And then before too long it was dinner and then after dinner we'd say: 'Well, we'll do it tomorrow', and the days just kept falling one after the other and we never made the calls.
HARRY: Then it struck us that no one knew where we were. We felt awkward. 'Course we did. It wasn't nice. We're the first to admit it. But we were in—well—
HENNY: The grip of something—
HARRY: That's just about it. We were in the grip of something. And we couldn't make ourselves get back to— We just couldn't have conversations. We kept thinking: how can we get out of this?
HENNY: I thought, well, we need time. That's all. And so we told my mother that if anyone asked, we were travelling. Just that. Just travelling.
HARRY: And the longer we stayed, the less reason there seemed to be to leave.

Beat.

JANE: Well, didn't you miss people?

HARRY *and* HENNY *look at each other.*

HENNY: Well, no. No we didn't. We just had this other— The need for company felt… quenched. We were enough for each other—
HARRY: The two of us and—
HENNY: And this other— Well, something else was holding us together—
JANE: Something—?
HENNY: A convivial kind of a feeling. A warm feeling. A sense of warmth—
EVE: What sort of feeling— What sort of 'warm feeling'?

HARRY: [*with a lightness, seemingly without understanding of the others' shock, caught up in the pleasantness*] It was like—you'll appreciate this!—when I first saw Henny—remember—at the girl who became the newsreader's twenty-first—
EVE: Lucy Wilmott.
HENNY: Lucy Wilmott!
EVE, HENNY & DAN: [*together*] With the pole!
HARRY: Yes. And you know— there was Henny in that blue dress talking to Ralph Langridge—
HENNY: [*smiling*] It wasn't Ralph— No! It was Martin Fennelly—
HARRY: So sure of herself, laughing—I *knew* she was the one. She made me feel— Well, what *was* that? Something of a giddiness—a lightness, together with never feeling more connected to the planet in my life. A sense of being more intensely myself than I had ever been and yet being *more* than my own self—
EVE: Love, then?
HARRY: Yes, like that. Only bigger.
HENNY: And it was the strangest thing, because until then we never really knew we'd been missing anything. And yet now that we felt this—
HARRY: This way—
HENNY: Now we knew that we'd been without—
HARRY: Just *without*—
HENNY: For the longest time.

> Beat.

HARRY: And then we got your call.
HENNY: You rang.
HARRY: I picked up the receiver and it was you. At first I wasn't sure—
HENNY: Seven months is a long time—
HARRY: But we realised that at a certain point, a choice had to be made.
HENNY: We had to make a choice.
HARRY: We sat there in the hotel and we realised it was either in here or—
HENNY: Out there.
HARRY: In here or out there.
HENNY: And it was time. It was time to go Out There.

> *Pause as they all take this in.*

DAN: [*struggling, giving it his best shot and then rambling hysterically realising it's too late to extricate himself*] Well, that's—that's— I guess that's good. I'm not sure that anyone can— I'm not sure it's something than anyone else can really experience in quite the same way. The thing is that we are all individuals and we feel things as individuals and there are individual responses and that's what makes life rich and interesting, the range of responses that human beings have to life's infinite complexity [*realising it's too late to go back*] and obviously this is your way of responding to your particular individual situation and that's a situation that we can relate to because we're—well—because we can *imagine* and we—well— we're roughly speaking from the same socio-economic and cultural background so while we can't be in there *with* you we can certainly be here *for* you and let you know that whatever individual experience you [*beginning to falter*] experience as individuals is respected by us as other individuals with our own—individual experience.

JANE: Nicely put.

TOM *is like a tiger. He's been quietly watching, thinking, absorbing, taking it in. And now he moves in:*

TOM: [*neutral*] You went away and then, without even looking for it, without even calling for it, something just 'woke up'?

HARRY: That's right. That's the gist of it.

TOM: [*still with no judgement*] That's the gist of it?

HARRY: Yes. Yes. More or less. I mean, it's more complicated than that.

TOM: [*neutrally*] It's more complicated, but that's the gist?

HARRY: Yes.

Beat.

TOM: [*with studied calm*] Let me just— Bear with me, I'm just trying to get a clear picture here. The Glamorous Gourmet and the Real Estate Agent of the Year—*celebrities*—of a kind in our fair city—experience a devastating loss when their glorious house burns down and find that as a result, they start feeling… *warm*. [*Beat.*] There's a light. There's a warm feeling. There's something 'beyond' something. It's all just like Henny twenty-five years ago at Lucy Wilmott's twenty-first. It's all about the Impossible Phoning of Friends.

DAN: Harry and Henny are confiding—they're telling us, in their own way, they're telling us something that is meaningful for them.

TOM: Something 'meaningful'?

JANE: It's still Harry and Henny. Isn't it? I mean, Henny. It's still you, isn't it?
HENNY: We're here. We're right here. We're exactly the same. *Only… better.*
   Beat.
TOM: I'm sorry. But clearly, for reasons not altogether evident, Harry and Henny, in the fullness of grief and without the aid of counsel, have *completely lost their minds.*
EVE: Tom!
TOM: [*to* HARRY *and* HENNY] *You're insane!*
JANE: Tom—
TOM: YOU'RE INSANE! [*Beat.*] And that's okay! [*Beat.*] *You're allowed to be.*
HARRY: Tom, we've never felt—
TOM: *I* know! *I* know! You're absolutely fine, it's just that you hear little voices in your head—
HARRY: *Saner.* Never.
TOM: I don't care if you've put little fish stickers all over your Volvo station-wagon, you two are not the kind of people—
HARRY: What kind of people?
TOM: The kind of people who believe that once upon a time a guy in a caftan went: 'Abracadabra'—
DAN: Now, Tom, that's just—
JANE: There's no need to—
HENNY: Good or evil, justice, fate? Why did our house burn, Tom?
TOM: Because some people are maniacs. Some people are fucked up and they like burning down houses, so some people's houses burn down. There is no point. There is no justice.
HENNY: What kind of world would it be—a world simply of physical forces and reproduction?
TOM: Not 'what kind of world would it be'—what kind of world *is* it? It's *our* kind of world.
DAN: Just calm down, Tom, just take it easy—
TOM: Don't tell me to take it easy! We're witnessing full-scale delusion!
HENNY: Delusion? Oh, goodness no, Tom.
TOM: 'Goodness no.' That's all you have to say?
HENNY: [*smiling gaily*] Well, it's just that it's funny—
TOM: It's funny?

HENNY: It's really *very* funny.
TOM: Funny, ha-ha, is it?
HENNY: [*sweetly delighted, not aggressive at all*] Yes, you see, because *we* think *you're* deluded!
TOM: For Christ's sake, Henny! You don't *do* this to your friends—
HENNY: Don't do what?
TOM: Change. [*Beat.*] All this bullshit about change being for the better, how great it is when people 'grow and change'. Have you noticed how change is invariably for the worse? Invariably! Think of Abba— You thought that was as bad as it could get and then there was *Chess*. Or George Bush the first. I mean, who would have thought there could be a *worse* George Bush?
HARRY: It's all right. Really. Because it's over. There's really nothing there, where the house was. There were things to say when the house was burning. But the fire's out.
TOM: Jesus Christ, Harry! You're a real estate agent—
EVE: Tom!
HARRY: You think property developers are excluded from spirituality?
TOM: Actually, yes. And believe me, I'm not alone.
EVE: Tom, you're not being—
HENNY: Well, you don't have to worry about that because he quit.
HARRY: Yes.
HENNY: He went and quit.
HARRY: Yes, I did.
EVE: [*shocked*] What?
HENNY: Harry's sold the business.
HARRY: I sold it, all right.
DAN: Jesus, Harry!
JANE: You sold the business?
HARRY: It wasn't difficult—
JANE: Harry, it was your *life*.
HARRY: Was it?
JANE: You lived to work!
HARRY: [*dead-pan*] For a long time I thought it was a reason for living and then I realised it was a real estate agency.
DAN: A year ago. The party!
TOM: Silver balloons dancing beneath the marquee roof. A lot of shiny men doing the Macarena—

HARRY: Yes, yes, shiny men—
TOM: Real Estate Agent of the Year! You can't dismiss that, Harry. I mean for men in pink satin ties and BMWs, it's pretty much it.
JANE: Oh, for God's sake, Tom!
HARRY: [*refusing to be baited*] I guess it is.
EVE: What about the show, Henny? And the books?
HENNY: I've decided not to do another series.
TOM: The Glamourous Gourmet bites the dust!
HENNY: I'm—well, I've had enough of it.
TOM: What? *Enough style?* I thought that was an oxymoron.
JANE: The network must be furious!
HENNY: It's not my job to keep the network happy.
TOM: Oh, no! No! Of course not. It's not your job to keep anyone happy. No, you just go along your merry way…
EVE: [*puzzled, gentle*] So what are you going to do?
TOM: [*belligerent, by contrast*] So what *are* you going to do? Go to Africa and convert the natives? Maybe you could head off to Club Med Zimbabwe? The pool-boys wear starched white uniforms which look too chic for words!
DAN: Tom—
HARRY: [*quiet, neutral*] Yes, well. We are travelling.

Beat.

TOM: [*disbelieving*] You're going to Africa?
HARRY: Actually, yes.
TOM: [*laughing madly*] Of course you are! Don't tell me! To work with little children?
HARRY: [*neutral*] With little children. Yes.
TOM: I don't fucking believe it!
EVE: Tom! For God's sake!
TOM: [*to* HARRY *and* HENNY] So what is it? What's the number one choice for middle-aged converts?
HARRY: We haven't joined anything—
TOM: Starting a new one, then? Good idea. So much more original than golf, and more fashion options!
DAN: Tom, for Christ's sake—
HARRY: Okay, well. This isn't really getting us anywhere.
HENNY: Maybe we should go.
EVE: Don't go!

HENNY: You know, it's really okay. This is about *us*. It's not about you. This isn't about choice. Something *called* us—
EVE: Something—?
HENNY: Yes—called us. And we answered.
JANE: Well. Well, *what?*
HENNY: What?
JANE: *What* called you?
   Beat.
HENNY: Well— [*Beat.*] A— [*Beat.*] A— [*Beat.*] Stillness.
JANE: A stillness?
HENNY: Yes. Yes. Stillness.
TOM: Called you? Yes. Oh, absolutely.
HENNY: It was a stillness.
JANE: What a—a beautiful idea.
TOM: Enchanting. But unfortunately they're lunatics.
HENNY: We're fine. We're absolutely fine.
TOM: You're fine and you've found—
HARRY: Nobody mentioned—
TOM: You've found—?
HARRY: *Ourselves*, Tom. Yes. We've found ourselves. And we like what we've found.
TOM: Oh, you do?
HARRY: Yes. Actually. Yes we do.
TOM: How *nice* for you.
HENNY: You're wrong about change, Tom. But I understand how frightening it must be—
TOM: I guess it's just a trifle unnerving when your best friends decide to run with wolves.
HENNY: Run with wolves? No, Tom. No. We saw a fox on the road near the Bedford turn-off. A fox. Not a wolf.
HARRY: And we swerved.
TOM: You swerved all right.
HENNY: And that was the beginning.
HARRY: Not exactly the beginning.
HENNY: Not exactly, but something like it.
HARRY: Something like the beginning.
TOM: [*trying hard*] Listen, I understand.
HARRY: Do you understand, Tom?

TOM: I'm your oldest friend.
HARRY: Yes, you are.
TOM: You've had a bad time. You've had a very bad time and you're going through something—
HARRY: No.
TOM: You're going through—
HARRY: We're not going *through* something, exactly. We're going *into* something.
TOM: You're going *into* something.
HARRY: Yes. That's fair. We're travelling into something and we're— well—
TOM: Go on—
HARRY: Well—
TOM: Say it!
HARRY: Well— [*Beat.*] We're not coming back.

SCENE THREE

EVE *and* JANE, DAN *and* TOM. *An almost whispering intensity, as if they've stolen a moment:*

JANE: It's all right. Really, Tom, it's all all right. We just have to get someone.
DAN: Get—? What—?
JANE: A cult-buster.
TOM: Oh, okay, I'll just pop down to Bunnings and get one!
EVE: What?
JANE: A cult-buster. You just get a house in the desert—
DAN: *What* desert?
JANE: *Any* desert! And you put Harry and Henny in there for a week with some TV dinners and a magnetically rational person like Harvey Keitel.
TOM: Oh, *good*. Oh, *excellent*. Somebody get Harvey Keitel on the phone.
DAN: We need to calm down. We all need to calm down.
JANE: They don't have children.
TOM: What?

32

JANE: That's the reason for this. They have too much time—
TOM: Very true!
JANE: I mean, what else have they got to do? If we didn't have children, *we'd* be climbing the Andes, wouldn't we?
EVE, DAN & TOM: [*together*] Of course we would!
JANE: I'm just putting it out there: a house in the desert.
TOM: That's helpful! That's terrific! Jane, get a grip! I don't think you realise what's at stake!
JANE: Maybe what's at stake is that finally you've come face to face with an argument that you can't win with words!
TOM: Believe me, I'd use martial arts if I could—
EVE: [*quietly, seeing the seriousness*] They're our friends.
TOM: What?
EVE: It wouldn't hurt, to listen, would it? To stop still, to allow some—*dignity*—?
TOM: Some—!
EVE: *They're our friends.*
DAN: Eve's right. We can't lose sight—
TOM: As if I needed—!
JANE: A house in the desert. That's all I'm saying. Ignore me if you wish.
EVE: It's no small thing. These—these—how many? How many? Twenty-five—*years*. Since that first summer?
DAN: Eve's right. I think 'empathy' is the word we should be summoning—
TOM: 'Empathy'?
DAN: Yes. Yes. It's an English word. It means 'feeling for others'.
JANE: Let's just calm down. Let's just— They'll be back in a second and we don't want them to—
EVE: These *are* our friends, aren't they, Tom. These people?

   Tiny beat.

TOM: Yes. Yes. They're our friends.
EVE: Maybe we should just listen to them?
TOM: Listen to them?
EVE: Yes. Yes. Imagine that.
DAN: [*to* TOM] Why do you care so much?
TOM: *Why do I care?*
DAN: It's a free world. If I want to declare my undying loyalty to the Easter Bunny, what's it to you?
TOM: Oh, so now you're going to tell me the Easter Bunny isn't real!

DAN: Why are you so upset?
TOM: Why *aren't* you? That's what you should be asking yourself. *Why aren't you upset?* Our closest friends have run completely off the rails and you don't give a damn—
DAN: If it makes them happy—
JANE: It *is* a private thing—
TOM: It's dished up as personal soul searching but it's a public declaration— Real change— Does it need a title? Does it need declaring? The decent thing is to become what it is one is becoming without making a fanfare—
EVE: You're the one making a fanfare!
DAN: Why do you care so much?
TOM: Because Harry and Henny have replaced us.
DAN: Nobody's been replaced!
TOM: Of course we have! You saw them—with their prissy little stoicism, perched on the sofa, neat, organised, resolved. How can anyone that resolved be spiritual, I ask you? It's arrogance masquerading as insider knowledge! Harry's never sounded so smug in his life! And faith's not some passive little decision— No! It's violent—
JANE: It is?
TOM: It's an act of hostility. Hostility. Hatred. And that's what—hurts—yes—hurts me. That Harry and Henny hate us that much—hate us so much that they can sit there smugly eating our rice crackers and tell us they've entered another world, a friendless cold world, and that they like it there *and they're never coming back.*
EVE: *You're* the one who's so smug! Why shouldn't they go to Africa? Why shouldn't they help little children?
TOM: What?!
EVE: That's all I want to know! Why shouldn't they help little children? What? [*Incredulous*] It offends your sense of originality?
TOM: What's gotten into you?
EVE: I'm not going to let you—
TOM: Let me—?
EVE: *Bully*—
TOM: Bully?
EVE: Me. No! Don't little children deserve to be noticed? What's *wrong* exactly with helping little children?
TOM: The world isn't going to turn into a lovely caring place because

two middle-aged yuppies frequent-fly to Addis Ababa.
EVE: Look at you! Look at you! Just think about it, Tom. Think about exactly what it is you make ridiculous.
TOM: You don't know what you're talking about. What *are* you talking about?
DAN: She's right! You're pulsating with certainty!
TOM: I'm not certain about anything. I'm an artist. I *explore* things!
DAN: Sure! Remember the bet?
TOM: What's that got to do—?
DAN: You were *sure*—
TOM: *Okay.*
DAN: You were so sure—you were—
TOM: Yes I was sure and I was wrong.
DAN: You had to buy a new car!
TOM: I wanted one anyway. You were doing me a favour.
DAN: *You bet your car, Tom.*
TOM: It's just a car. That's all it is. A car.
DAN: Because you were certain. I like the car. It's a good car.
TOM: [*unable to pretend; with love and regret*] It's a great car. It glides. They don't make cars like that anymore—the wooden interior— It's stately. Where are the stately cars? I'll tell you where: *nowhere.* Because they can make faster, stronger, smoother but they can't make *stately.* There are no more movie stars! No. There are no more movie stars. Because there are no more movie star cars. The cars *make* the stars.
DAN: It's a stately car. And it's *my* car.
TOM: It's your car.
DAN: Because you *refused*—
TOM: Well, really, I mean who would accept a car? Who would accept a car as a result of winning a bet?
DAN: Well. *I* would.
TOM: Obviously.
JANE: It was a fair bet. He—he urged you not to, but you were stubborn—
TOM: Well. I stick to my guns. That's an admired trait in some cultures.
DAN: So is eating your first cousin. You cried when you gave me the keys—
TOM: I didn't think you'd take it—
DAN: No, you didn't.

TOM: I didn't—
DAN: But I *did* take it. I didn't need a car, Tom.
JANE: He had a car.
DAN: I liked my car. But I took it because you made me mad. You're so fucking arrogant!
TOM: Excuse me, excuse me for placing some emphasis on the facts—
DAN: The facts? Maybe 'the facts' aren't the be-all and end-all, Tom!
TOM: What? [*Beat.*] You're— [*Astonished*] You're—? No! You're telling me— You—
DAN: I'm saying that between what you know and what actually exists, there may be a small space—
TOM: The facts: 'Not the be-all and end-all'? Are you insane? Throw a few words at you, did they? Light. Tunnels. That kind of thing?
DAN: Maybe the facts aren't enough for people! Maybe people need comfort!
TOM: Comfort?! Who the fuck *cares* what people need? Since when did people's *needs* dictate the truth? The truth *should* be comforting. *The truth is beautiful!*
DAN: In the end, what does it matter? It's their life, isn't it?
TOM: [*aghast*] What does it matter? *What does it matter?* It matters *a lot*. It matters *significantly*. Because it makes them one of 'the others'.
JANE: Maybe 'the others' aren't so bad!
TOM: If you took the one common denominator of the neo-Nazis and the Arabs and the African tin-pot dictators, you'd get faith. When they hold auditions for fucked-up lunatics, the first question they ask is: 'Are you a Believer?' But this is totally predictable! I should have seen it coming.
DAN: Seen *what* coming?
TOM: You and your 'understanding'. You define yourself by being likeable!
DAN: Oh, so that's wrong! To be likeable is *wrong?*
TOM: You want everyone to like you.
EVE: Everyone *does* like him.
TOM: You can't stand being disliked. You— It's as if you evaporate—
DAN: You're really being absurd now!
TOM: You would never hold a conviction higher than your willingness to be unanimously approved of. A psychotic obsession with making people like you! You rationalise your way out of any personal instinct that might isolate you. You unconsciously shift that instinct to make

yourself amenable.
DAN: Maybe that's my ultimate ambition! Maybe there's something noble in that. To be amenable.
TOM: I'd rather be shot in the head than described as amenable!
DAN: [*furious and embarrassed*] I'm sure that could be arranged.
JANE: Amenable people are capable of moving outside of their own selfish needs.
TOM: Now you're calling me selfish!
JANE: Yes I am!
TOM: I'm selfish enough to give you a sizeable donation to make a fucking film about Geoffrey Rush's sister that no one in their right mind would want to see!
EVE: What?
DAN: You *are* selfish! And you're envious! That people like me and they *don't* like—
TOM: What!
DAN: They *don't* like you! Nobody likes you.
EVE: I sort of like him.
DAN: *You have* to. [*To* TOM] As Talbot Jones says: 'You're a mosaic of late twentieth-century Western literary styles— A master of the art of camouflaging your own sheer impenetrable unpleasantness in a flurry of nattily articulated style.'
TOM: What instant recall you have—
DAN: I defended you, but we both know he's right! You don't have to believe to respect belief. You don't know what 'reaching out' to someone means.
TOM: It means you're a sycophant!
DAN: Who do you care about, Tom? Who on Earth do you care about?
TOM: For your information, I empathise on a professional basis! It's my *job* to put myself in other people's shoes and in case you've forgotten I've even won prizes for it! While you write your little columns, I'm empathising my way through three fucking volumes of award-winning prose!

> HARRY *and* HENNY *enter from the kitchen as* TOM *finishes, unseen by the others.* HENNY *is holding a tray with nibbles, napkins, etc. They watch silently, still, as the scene ends.*

DAN: [*quietly and with feeling*] You know, you have a duty of care, Tom. You have great things. You have good fortune. But you have no grace.

EVE *looks at* DAN *carefully, with gratitude.*

TOM: Grace? What?

DAN: You ought to be more grateful.

TOM: More grateful for what?

Momentary blackout.

SCENE FOUR

Lights up: EVE, TOM, DAN, JANE *as they were,* HARRY *and* HENNY *move towards them from the kitchen door.*

HENNY: We found some dip.
TOM: What?
HENNY: Dip.
JANE: Dip?
HENNY: Yes. In the fridge.
TOM: [*vacantly*] Dip. Excellent.
EVE: Oh, yes. The dip.
DAN: [*serious, absent*] Well done. That's what we need. Dip.

As HENNY *lowers the tray onto the coffee table,* HARRY *has taken a seat in an armchair, with an air of steadfast settling-in. There's a lull while the others automatically and disinterestedly eat dip and then* HARRY *starts speaking out of nothing.*

HARRY: [*unprovoked, wanting him to understand*] Do you know what it's like, Tom—to feel pure joy? To sit on a motel step with your wife and feel a deep, magnificent, infinite sense of peace? Could you imagine that, Tom? Could any of you even imagine that?

TOM: Listen, Harry. I love my wife. I dig my job. I've procreated. I live in a nice house. Above that, it's enjoyable to like things, to whine about things and even to actively dislike things, because envy and impatience and sheer ordinary meanness are what it is to be human, along with the capacity to love and the inability to choose well from the menu or finish *Illywhacker*. Joy is a fictitious state dreamt up by nice, well-dressed people who underneath it all are *completely freaking out*.

HARRY: [*quiet, calm, neutral*] It's not enough, Tom.

TOM: *What* isn't enough, Harry?

HARRY: All of it. It took me a while, but finally it clicked. It's not enough for me to sell people houses, Tom. It's not enough for me to make a couple of hundred grand a year.

TOM: We all have those thoughts! Of course we do! But we get over them!

HARRY: *I don't want to get over them.* [*Beat.*] You know, we built that deck, Tom. You and me and Dan.

TOM: Yes, we did.

HARRY: We built that deck. Remember, Dan?

DAN: Yes, Harry, I do.

HARRY: I pictured it just the way I wanted it. The French doors opening onto the deck, and then looking out to the pond through the avenue of birches. Remember, we had to redo the right side? I made you pull up the planks. Even though it was forty degrees.

TOM: I could have killed you. I nearly did.

HARRY: [*sadly*] That was my house. That was my deck.

Beat.

TOM: [*gentle*] What's going on, Harry?

HARRY: The thing is, I don't feel certain about things, anymore. And I've been struggling with this for—well, for—a sense that I just don't know what's going to happen.

TOM: What's going to happen?

HARRY: Yes. I mean. We keep trying to manage things, to manage them. We try to stop things from surprising us, but they do. They do.

HENNY: You turn a bend in the road and your house is gone.

EVE: The phone rings.

HARRY: Exactly.

EVE: The phone rings, and—

HARRY: Exactly.

HENNY: It's the strangest thing. How a person's apparent undoing can actually rescue them. We dread… we spend so much of our lives dreading, in dread, fearing what might happen, never realising that if we embraced disaster, we might be free of it.

HARRY: Something happens when you stop demanding certainty—
DAN: Something—?
HARRY: Yes. Something happens when you just sit down with uncertainty and look it in the eye. [*Beat.*] We use things—we find strategies—
DAN: Strategies?
HARRY: For managing the tininess—
DAN: For managing—
HARRY: *Our* tininess. Book deals, television contracts, dinner parties. We confuse ourselves to keep the knowledge at bay—
DAN: The knowledge—
HARRY: That it's here and then it's over. It's a simple thing, but somehow intolerable. So we manufacture our diversions and sometimes we can do that for… well, for as long as we have. I spent a long time pointing out attractive features—
DAN: Yes—
HARRY: A picturesque gazebo. Architraves. A northerly aspect. And for a long time, it worked. I *cared* about architraves—
DAN: You cared, Harry—
HARRY: And then I didn't.
DAN: It stopped working.
HARRY: I can sell things. I'm *good* at selling things. But at a certain point one has to ask oneself what it is one is selling. You make a choice. You stop and say: 'Enough of that. If it's got a roof, it's a house.' You know what I'm saying—?
TOM: This from the fellow who's been Chez Grand Hyatt.
HARRY: It's got a roof, Tom—
TOM: And three TVs!
HARRY: It's just a place to stay. We were there a couple of days before it didn't mean a damn thing. We realised we've got this much time. So we're going to make a point of all this. It's going to be a real point.
DAN: Yes.
HARRY: Do you know what's real, Dan?

  EVE *watches him closely.*

DAN: Love is real.
TOM: Oh, good. Now *you're* sounding like a Coke commercial.
DAN: Love is real. [*To anyone*] Isn't it?
EVE: Yes.

DAN: [*sorting this out as he speaks*] You live your whole life stifling the one thing that actually makes sense of things. Real artists try to tap that. But the rest of us—we're frightened of what makes us cry out— We summon the sound then just at the brink, we muffle it. The cry of life. We pull it back and swallow it. We say only what can be said neatly. [*Beat.*] Why is that? We defer to mediocrity, over and over again, trying to put passion in its place instead of using it—
TOM: What's gotten into everyone?
DAN: We just—accept the... the agony. Because other things take precedence—order, certainty, but what is it we lose? What do we lose when we kill off the cry of life, the heart of us? Is it better to be orderly? I don't know. Is it better to hide behind a tidy exterior?
TOM: Believe me, facades are greatly under-rated!
DAN: Or do we claim our passions, despite the madness or disaster they provoke, because otherwise they wear away at us, they wear away at us and leave us... bereft?

Beat as EVE *studies him.*

TOM: 'Passions'! You have passions, do you, Dan?
DAN: [*with suffering*] One or two.

EVE *is greatly affected by this.*

EVE: There has to be a reason—in the face of it—in the face of all the arguments *against*— There has to be a reason why people instinctively turn—towards—
TOM: [*confused, cross*] Eve?
EVE: Towards some sense of— Towards mystery.
TOM: [*urgent, demanding*] Why is mystery more compelling than science?
EVE: [*she's discovering something*] Because knowledge cannot answer feeling. The mere fact of something is not enough. Is it Henny?
HENNY: That's right.
EVE: [*realising, almost to herself*] The disappointment with fact. That is what faith is.
TOM: [*irritated*] What are you talking about? The trouble is, Eve, you can't think clearly. You just can't think clearly. You never have been able to.
EVE: How lovely it must be. To just let go and just own the truth instead of always trying to hold it down.

TOM: What 'truth'? You've had too much to drink and nothing to eat. It's all burnt. [*Looking at* HENNY *and* HARRY] And who's fault is that?

EVE: [*quietly, gathering strength again*] If we went on—all of us—the way we are—what really would we have? The world with all its—all its— The world out there would just get bigger and bigger, while we at our dining table start to shrink. At first, closing the doors, drawing the curtains, then, slowly, slowly pushing the furniture up against the walls, building it higher, barricading ourselves in. In here. In here with our TV and our books.

TOM: I *like* our TV and our books.

EVE: I know you do. They're… gorgeous.

JANE: We all like them.

HENNY: But at a certain point, you have to make a choice, Tom. It's in here, or—

HARRY: Out there.

EVE: And at a certain point, if we stay here, in here at our dinner party, we won't be able to leave. There won't be any way out. The books will pile up… biographies… novels…

HENNY: Cook books.

EVE: And it will just be us. With the books getting higher and higher—and the TV.

TOM: I like the TV. I like it in here. It's better than out there.

HENNY: That's what we thought. But Harry and I—we realised—all of us—we need to be—*connected*—

EVE: The books piling up… Thousands of books… Channel-surfing our way towards death… What if faith is just the willingness to venture out—?

TOM: 'Out'?

EVE: From where it's safe.

HARRY: What if faith is simply the personal capacity to struggle with issues of rightness—

TOM: Of rightness? You think morality is owned by the spiritually enlightened? See, this really *annoys* me. For your information, there are people out there, people like—ah, let me think, like *me* for instance, who care deeply about doing the right thing without murdering their rational selves.

HARRY: Who care deeply about doing the right thing?
TOM: Yes!
HARRY: [*with casual penetration*] But do you do it? [*Beat. Gentle, unprovoked*] I know it sounds naïve. But I don't mind. The proof is in the doing. If I do something valuable, it will demonstrate that my word carries weight.
TOM: You don't have to prove that. I know that.
HARRY: Not to other people, Tom. To myself. For a while now, I haven't really trusted that.
TOM: What do you mean?
HARRY: Before the fire... I started to have these random thoughts about— About goodness.
EVE: About—?
HARRY: Yes. *Goodness*. I'd be going about ordinary life, going to work, going out, and I started to feel troubled. The first time it happened, I was driving to *Annie*—
JANE: Who's Annie?
HARRY: The musical. We were given tickets. I was at a stop-light. A fellow was making his way across the road in his wheelchair and he had to try a couple of times before he got over the kerb onto the pavement. It sounds silly, but I started crying.
TOM: That was helpful.
HARRY: I just started crying. I couldn't go on.
TOM: I guess that's the price you pay for compassion. Two seats to *Annie*.
HARRY: [*ignoring him, caught up in the memory*] I pulled over and I wept and I realised I needed to—*do* something—
JANE: Do—? What—?
HARRY: I'd watch the news or read the paper and instead of feeling badly about what I saw and moving on, moving on and getting on, I'd stay with it. I found myself dwelling—
EVE: Dwelling on—
HARRY: The idea that each one of us has— We are all of us equipped with powers—
TOM: Oh, good. Oh, hello Kryptonite.
HARRY: Actually, just the ordinary capacity to alter outcomes.
EVE: [*quietly excited*] Yes, Harry! Yes.

This section has an urgency to it. A still urgency to HARRY. *An agitated urgency to* TOM.

HARRY: I'd think to myself: Something simply must be done. I must *do* something. But the next day I'd find myself driving around the inner-suburbs showing young lawyers apartments with European appliances as if nothing had happened. I realised I was incapable of taking myself seriously. Well, I've had enough of that. I need to believe in my own word again, before I die.

TOM: You're forty-six, Harry—

HARRY: But I could very well go on feeling things and burying them under the weight of daily life—I could do that for another forty years, but I'm tired of feeling cynical, Tom. It's a depressing emotion.

TOM: But you want all of us—to do the same thing. You're *implying* that we—

HARRY: No—

TOM: That we should all give ourselves over to—to 'goodness'.

HARRY: [*with quiet steadiness*] Well. Well. Even if that were true, would that be a bad thing?

TOM: I think I see… Yes… I think I *do* see. This 'otherness'—this silence, stillness—it's an insurance scheme—to ensure that if there is life beyond, you and Henny will be well looked after— You'll be put up at the Grand Hyatt of the afterlife— It's goodness *for a point*—

HENNY: For a point, Tom?

TOM: Yes, Henny. For a point.

HENNY: Well, there is a point, but it's not that, Tom. Whether there is or isn't anything beyond—and frankly if they can export Tasmanian lettuce to Shanghai I don't see why there shouldn't be an afterlife— but whether or not there is, we're simply talking about respect.

TOM: [*urgently*] Look, I'm sorry. I don't think I'm a bad person. I'm happy to pay my taxes and build homeless shelters, but the fact is I don't want to be at the coalface. I like what I do. I'm good at what I do.

HARRY: [*calmly*] The thing is Tom, you have some idea that you're striding through life on your own. You're not alone.

TOM: I have a wife. I have a daughter.

HARRY: No. I mean all of us. All of us. We're here with you.

TOM: All of whom?

HARRY: Well, everyone. Those people in the homeless shelters. They're not just a problem. They're actual people.

TOM: I realise that.

HARRY: I'm not sure that you do. We need to be thinking about the power we have to turn things around. And the duty we have to exercise that power.
TOM: I do my turning around with words.
HARRY: With words, Tom?
TOM: Yes, Harry. With words. You know my book won the prize?
HENNY: Yes. Yes, we read about it.
> Beat.
TOM: [*astonished*] That's it?
> Beat. JANE *starts laughing. She finds this desperately funny.*
JANE: [*laughing*] 'That's it?' [*Laughing*] 'That's it?'
> *The others turn to look at her and she stops.*
EVE: [*quietly, and quietly building*] You do your—? You do—? With words? You think—that with the right adjective you might—you might cause some—alteration? Cures lighted upon? Presidents toppled? Borders refixed? Through—through *words?*
TOM: That's enough, Eve!
EVE: The conviction of the writer… What a wondrous thing… Years ago—I believed a writer might occupy some place, a higher place, where the vision was more truthful, but now I see it's just more elegant—
TOM: And you despise elegance, don't you, Eve?! With your elegant house and your elegant clothes and your elegant fucking book club!
EVE: You're frightened! You're frightened and you can't bear it!
TOM: I'm frightened you— You've *caught* something—
EVE: Maybe I've caught something good!
TOM: You're making a fool of yourself!
EVE: You know for a while we saw you as our Best Version. But can you feel the fear creeping in here, minute by minute, the fear that you *are* our best version? With your declarations of decency as if you can *state* your way into righteousness! How terrifying if each of us *is* no better than you. No wonder Harry and Henny have come to leave us! They're running… they're running as fast as they can! And if they run fast enough, they may succeed in losing sight…
TOM: I think you've said quite enough!
EVE: Not *quite* enough. Tell me this, when we've said our goodnights, made our melancholy love—rare though it is—when we've called

45

a halt to the loose ends of a day, do you ever just surrender to the silence? Give in to its… length and breadth…? Do you know *how* to surrender?

TOM: Surrender? [*Beat.*] What?

EVE: [*building*] Who *are* you?

TOM: What?

EVE: Who are you? [*Beat.*] I don't know who you are. *Who are you?*

TOM: Eve?

EVE: [*with tremendous rage*] THERE'S A LITTLE GIRL AT MY MOTHER'S HOUSE. THERE'S A LITTLE GIRL. SHE'S WAITING FOR YOU.

TOM: What are you talking about?

EVE: SHE'S BEEN WAITING FOR HOURS. HOURS AND HOURS. DAYS. WEEKS. YEARS. SHE'S BEEN WAITING FOR YOU. UP THE STAIRS. IN HER ROOM. WAITING FOR YOU.

TOM: Eve!

EVE: Your child.

TOM: Yes!

EVE: SAY IT!

TOM: My child. All right?

EVE: SAY IT! SAY IT!

TOM: MY CHILD. *MY CHILD!*

    EVE and TOM *are both shocked by what has passed between them.*

[*To* HENNY, *with exasperation and the beginnings of fear*] Do you see what you're doing? Do you see what's happening? You're driving us all mad! You're pulling us *all* into your—

HENNY: No one is forcing you to come with us, Tom. We're not telling you what's right for any of you—

TOM: Yes you are! Yes you are! People like you— You ram this down our— You put this in front of us and you *force*—

HENNY: We're not forcing anything—

TOM: You *force* us to make a decision. We come with you or we don't and the implication is that if we don't—we live in a kind of happy idiocy, lost in the world of material comforts, caring about our cars and our children's schools and we have no idea—about meaning or—or—'the point'. This isn't about you—this is about us. It's about how *we're* not good enough for *you.*

HARRY: Questions had to be asked.

TOM: [*complete shift in tone, suddenly, sadly*] Harry, I love you.

HARRY: Well, well—

TOM: I love you.

HARRY: Well, [*Beat.*] Thank you.

TOM: [*sweetly, quietly*] I've known you since I was six years old. Now, all of a sudden I don't meet with your approval?

HARRY: It's not that we don't approve. Not at all. Who are we to approve or disapprove? It's more a question of like. Of like. And no one was more surprised than us to find that when we faced things—square on—we… well… we *didn't* like—

TOM: [*confused*] You—didn't—?

HENNY: There are some alterations that… friendship finds difficult—to accommodate. And that's really all right, because who's to say that friendships are 'built to last'?

TOM: [*sadly, stunned*] Henny, I gave you away.

HENNY: [*a moment of real sadness taking her by surprise*] Yes, Tom.

TOM: I gave you away.

 HENNY *loses her composure for a moment, feels the sorrow of all that is lost, then resurrects her composed self.*

HENNY: I know you did, Tom. But once something is glimpsed—well—the harder one tries not to see it, the more impossible it becomes to avoid—and we looked at you all and saw—

TOM: What? What did you see?

HENNY: Perhaps that doesn't need— We should go—

 HARRY *and* HENNY *stand.*

HARRY: We should go. It's late.

TOM: No! I'm sure Travis doesn't mind waiting up!

HENNY: Tom— It's late—

HARRY: We're tired. We're tired and we're hungry.

TOM: I'm sure room service is twenty-four hours! You can have your Caesar Salad in a minute. BUT I'M YOUR FRIEND. I'M YOUR OLDEST FRIEND AND YOU'RE NOT LEAVING THIS HOUSE UNTIL YOU SAY WHAT IT IS YOU SAW.

 HENNY *and* HARRY *look at* TOM, *then at each other. They sit. Long beat.*

HARRY: You know, Tom, a while ago I got it that really what you were all about was delivery. For you, delivery is always more important than content, something that literary prize judges may not be aware of, but to those of us who know you best, a clear thing. Cynicism. This is really your faith. And so addicted are you to the tone, you forget to concern yourself with the substance. It would never occur to you to ponder the merits of a life dedicated to others. Because you prefer the cheap thrill of your own tinkling, cynical dismay—the performance, the whole performance.

HENNY: The things that are noticed—in friendships—the things that are noticed—well—

HARRY: They can't be denied. Not really. Because they wear away, they wear away. I mean, we honour you with the truth—

TOM: The truth?

HARRY: And we believe you should honour us in the same way.

TOM: [*disbelieving, confused*] For forty years, I've been good enough for you.

HARRY: But Tom, I'm not who I was then. If we met now—we wouldn't—

TOM: We wouldn't—?

HARRY: No. We've been caught in the momentum of acquaintance.

TOM: *Acquaintance?*

HARRY: All of us.

TOM: [*confused, sad*] This is it? This is where all these years have—? This is the finale to all those birthdays and anniversaries, the children's parties, the summer house, the acquisitions, inspecting new cars and paintings—dead parents, cancer scares, cartons of photographs… There we are, flash-framed with arms around shoulders, relishing the familiarity we offer one another when all around… when all around… is darkness and strangeness and fear. There we were. All of us. You're telling me that you can just throw that away?

HARRY: We're not throwing it away, Tom. We're giving it back.

TOM: [*resurrecting himself*] YOU'RE GIVING IT BACK? WELL, GUESS WHAT? YOU CAN'T GIVE IT BACK! *YOU CAN'T GIVE IT BACK!* AND I DON'T WANT IT. I DON'T WANT IT BACK. I DON'T WANT THE YEARS BACK. THE WEDDINGS, THE CHILDREN, THE BUILDING OF DECKS. ALL OF IT. IF YOU DON'T WANT IT YOU HAD BETTER GET RID OF IT YOURSELF BECAUSE *I'M NOT TAKING IT.* YOU COME IN HERE—YOU COME INTO THIS HOUSE AND YOU JUST DEPOSIT YOUR—YOUR—FAITH—HERE AT OUR FEET? YOU JUST DUMP YOUR FAITH HERE? YOU JUST EXPECT US TO SAY OKAY WELL FINE, FINE, EACH TO HIS

OWN? WELL, NO! NO! *NOT* EACH TO HIS OWN. EACH TO *ALL OF US.* EACH TO ALL OF US!

Long beat. The moment is over. He gathers himself:

You know, quite a lot of people think this life is okay. Quite a lot of people think we're good people. Some people even think my books are good.

JANE: [*quietly*] But at whose expense?

TOM: What?

JANE: At whose expense?

Beat.

TOM: [*absorbing her meaning*] I *imagine* things.

JANE: You made a fool of me, Tom.

TOM: We've been through this, Janie. It's not you.

JANE: For Christ's sake, Tom! Your protagonist is a forty-year-old documentary film-maker and *I'm* a forty-year-old documentary film-maker—

TOM: *Aspiring*—

JANE: I've made films!

TOM: They were three and a half minutes long, Jane!

JANE: You plagiarised—

TOM: I've never plagiarised in my life!

DAN: You plagiarised *her* life!

JANE: I trusted you— [*Not point scoring, with genuine distress*] Tom. *Tom. I trusted you.*

TOM: [*admitting*] I'm a writer, Jane. That's what I do. If you're in a writer's field of vision—you have to *expect*—

JANE: Do you? Do you, Tom? That's just the modus operandi? Betraying trust—?

TOM: Betraying trust or betraying the work— How you make that judgement is what *makes* you a writer—

JANE: How—how lonely that must be. [*Beat.*] I must be naïve— I must be—somehow ridiculous—because I simply thought it—*unkind*—

TOM: [*balancing discomfort with justification*] Well, perhaps it *was* unkind. Perhaps it was. But do you know—maybe it's more unkind to allow you to perpetuate the belief—

EVE: Tom!

TOM: That you have an ounce of creativity. Jane, you are no artist.

JANE: And you are no friend. [*Beat.*] The irony is I actually do— [*Impossible to say*] I do— [*Beat.*] There was one moment—one moment in all the years—that night, when Dan and I had a fight and I didn't know where he was and I rang you. Remember?

TOM: I came over in the hailstorm.

JANE: Eddie was two. And you got drunk with me.

TOM: On Long Island Teas.

JANE: And you held him against your chest. And every so often, I go back to that image of you in the old blue armchair with Eddie's fat little arms around your neck and I think, somewhere that person is inside you... [*Beat.*] Better not to have known that. Better never to have known it, than to mourn it. [*Beat.*] You're going to wake up one day and find that nobody is left.

TOM: I don't know what you're talking about. Dan? Dan? What *is* she talking about?

DAN: I don't know.

JANE: Come on, Dan! Come on!

DAN: I don't know what you're talking about.

EVE *looks at* JANE *with particular intensity.*

EVE: Go on, then. Say it. Say it!

JANE: [*rising to her*] You think I won't?

EVE: Say it!

JANE: You think I'll defer again? Again and again? Defer to my admiration for you?

DAN: Jane!

JANE: [*to* EVE, *undeterred*] Since the very beginning, I *longed* for your respect, knowing it was just a fraction out of reach. You smiled at me so benevolently, dispensing your enigmatic charm but never quite admitting me as equal— Why did it matter to me?

EVE: [*hard, defensive*] Why *did* it matter to you?

JANE: Because there are things about you that are—that *are*—miraculous. And tragically, tragically, I thought that my silence might earn your—

TOM: What are you talking about?

JANE: But I am not the reason he stayed, am I? He stayed out of duty, because he actually *believes* in duty.

TOM: Will somebody—?

EVE: [*hard, to* JANE] *Say it!*

Beat.

JANE: It's a strange sort of thing, to be married to a man in love with someone else.

TOM: What?

JANE: [*continuing on her own track*] You respect the size of what they feel at the same time as regretting that your loss is someone else's gain.

DAN: It's not over—

JANE: The vanishing of love only goes to glamorise love that thrives—a husband's love, but not for… not for… Your whole breathing, sleeping, working existence becomes captive to the gloriousness of something that has been stolen from you.

EVE: [*feeling for her*] Jane—I never stole—

JANE: [*with utter conviction*] But you would have, if you'd had to.

TOM: Is this—? Eve? Eve? Is this—?

JANE: Who can blame anyone for who they love and who they don't? It's not a choice. *I* would love Eve over me. Yes. Who wouldn't? The way she moves her hand to push her hair aside? The way she teams things—the patterned tights, the silk scarf, the bakelite bracelet. I mean, it's the little things, isn't it? That make for passion? And in the end, who can fight the magnificent wrongness of adulterous passion? It has to win! It *has* to win!

DAN: Nothing's—no—happened.

EVE: Hasn't it?

JANE: Skin, bones, lips, eyes, they don't bother me so much as… the growing sense that *I'm* the enemy…

TOM: Will somebody please—?

JANE: [*to* DAN] Once I actually believed in long-distance love. Isn't that odd? It always seemed to me that infidelity, however brilliant, was ultimately Love-Lite. And if you could only hang on, hang on until it flared and died out, the real thing would come into its own. And sometimes, to comfort myself, I think back to that night—nineteen years ago—at that fucking awful dinner party when we looked at each other for the first time—in silent conspiracy—allying ourselves over lemon tart and fourteen gossiping stockbrokers listening to Wham!— All this time I've been trying to regain that moment, that flirtatious, daring glance between us. *A glance.* Isn't that sad? We built a *life* out of that glance—a house, a child—never realising that the glance itself was the pinnacle.

DAN: Jane, I do—

Silence. He can't finish the sentence.

JANE: [*quietly*] Go on, then. Say it.

DAN: I do—

Silence. He can't say it. Both distraught.

TOM: [*shocked, quiet*] Eve?

She says nothing.

Really? Really, Eve?

Silence.

Eve?

Her eyes answer his question. He is shocked, dismayed, utterly destroyed. Long beat.

HENNY: The thing is, one asks oneself, in these moments, one asks oneself if one deserves—

JANE: Deserves—?

HENNY: Something more. [*Beat.*] Or if one should just go along with things.

JANE: Something more than love?

HENNY: Love? Is it? If it's love, then it's a scornful love.

DAN: 'Scornful?'

HENNY: That's what I'd call it. Is that what you'd call it, Harry?

HARRY: 'Scornful' love? Yes. Yes. Scornful.

DAN: What?

HENNY: And that's perhaps what you need to ask yourself, Jane. Do you deserve more than a scornful love?

DAN: [*shocked*] Henny?

HARRY: There are those who act and those who are acted upon.

DAN: [*stunned*] What? What are you—? Who are you to speak of—? How dare you! Walk in here—walk into a place of—of *friendship*—parading your *consciences!* Your superiority! How dare you!

HARRY: We do dare. Yes. We just do dare.

DAN: This is nothing to do with you! Nothing to do with you and your faith! This is about *us*—

EVE: It's not about you!

DAN: How dare you walk in here and start *judging!*
HARRY: Actually—actually, Dan—with time, you'll thank us.
DAN: Thank you?! For coming back here, with your revelations, with your self-importance? Working away at other people's business—
HENNY: While you were working away at other people's wives?
DAN: [*with burgeoning wonder*] I never realised... how brutal you could be. You two. There's something—*savage.*
HENNY: Savage? Yes. Yes! The truth *is* savage. Yes. As Tom reminded us, that's what *makes* it the truth!
HARRY: She's right. If you'd just listen. If you'd all just listen.
HENNY: That's the beauty of it. Everything you're running from. You need to just look it square in the eye.
HARRY: That's exactly right.
HENNY: You need to take a long, hard look, like us. Like we did. And then... Well, it's beautiful.
HARRY: It *is* beautiful.
HENNY: It's a relief.
   Beat.
TOM: [*quiet, disbelieving, to* DAN] You'd take her?
DAN: [*liberated from niceness*] I *long* for her. I want to *taste* her. I want to trace every part of her, follow every dip and rise, discover her, surrender to her, claim her, make myself indistinguishable. *I want to lose myself in your wife.* Yes. Yes. I *long* for her. Sitting here alone, some Persian rugs for company. Mother to a child whose father has abandoned her for a bunch of headlines on the literary pages... *You* had her! *You* had her! But *I* loved her... The Oracle, too. A daughter too unwieldy to love... So you camouflaged her—camouflaged that child in— [*Beat.*] *In dinner parties.* In the background, the unrelenting hum of a difficult child's silence. Never here, never quite given away...
TOM: You were my friend.
DAN: Yes. Yes, Tom. I was. But after a while, when you wake up to the day and think: What? What? This *again?* This *again,* with its silences and little jokes to defend us against the absence of feeling... You start to ask, surely, surely, there *has* to be something more.
TOM: There's nothing more.
HENNY: There's something more. There's a lot more.
DAN: In all this time, you never realised how sorry I felt for you. That

you couldn't take pleasure from what exceeded your own outline. I always felt pity for you and that pity allowed me to love you... But you're right, Tom. There comes a time for the truth and it should be comforting... What it doesn't destroy, it strengthens...

TOM: [*destroyed*] Eve—?

EVE: You cannot survive a child like that without feeling—the deepest love or hate for one another. The intensity of her requires—something terrifying. [*Beat.*] I sit here with my thoughts, day after day, floating between these satellites: you, The Oracle, friends—thinking—thinking—how can anything ever change? Because one tiny change is all it takes for everything to change, but a tiny change is not so—not so—easy... I watch—this is the thing—other mothers who simply get on with mothering. That's what—well, what mothers are, they are stoics. They do what must be done. That's why—well, you hear women—they complain about their husbands going to work saying: 'Well, work is such a cinch, such a cinch compared to this.' And that's because we know that *our* failures amount to something so much greater— There, in amongst *The Bold and the Beautiful* and the bunny-rugs, our motion adds up to the most bizarre and exquisite mystery, the mystery of human life. And some women—well—in the face of this—some women—simply go—mad. Mad. Yes. [*Beat.*] I looked at that baby girl and sometimes it flashed upon me that I could end that life. To stare at something you love too much—and to think of the world outside that door—the endless disappointments... They begin, you see—or we begin—all of us—in a state of instinctive optimism. Hopeful. We approach the bouncing on the knee, the mother's breast, the elephant rattle, our father's homecoming at the end of the day—we approach these things with such anticipation and pleasure, and gradually, as a day turns to days and a year turns to years, we adjust. Until one day, we say: 'What tiny thing is left for me to find hope in?' And I would stare at the baby and the baby would remind me that I was once a baby and of all the things that have happened to me since I drank at my mother's breast, and I would think after this, she's heading for homicidal maniacs in hamburger restaurants and pedants and bores and illness and terror. And terror. And terror. And for a second the idea would flash across me—a pillow, a window, a fall—and to me, it was the women who *never* thought such things—who never trembled at the weight—at the size of the day, within those walls, the two of us, the house filling up with the sound of *her* heartbeat and the sound of *my* terror—the women who never thought like that—to me, *they* were the mad ones, chatting in the supermarket—never facing the terror—*they* were the mad ones and only the sad women—only *those* women were the sane ones. Only *they* understood what it was—the size of what it was they had to do. [*Beat.*] For years we've been terrified of her power, in *denial* of her power—

TOM: Evie— No—

EVE: That look, that cold, cold look—having dinner when she turns and puts her eyes on us. And it's clear there—iridescent—that she sees in us two people prepared to live a life without—finally, without due care—a careless life—a life of all surfaces, gorgeous surfaces, nicely laid tables ... and friends who see their own reflections in our gleaming silver and feel pleased to be a part of it.

HENNY: [*generally; to* DAN, JANE *and* HARRY] That's us. She's talking about us.

HARRY: 'The friends.' That's where we come in.

EVE: [*as if uninterrupted*] And then along come Henny and Harry, through the flames that lick at houses, who say, finally: 'We want to make a point.' Henny's 'inventory of significant losses'—in the end—isn't that what a life amounts to? And who could blame them for searching for an antidote to that?

TOM: An inventory of losses? Is that all our life is? [*Beat. Reluctantly, quietly*] The thing is, I don't much like life unwritten, Evie.

EVE: No.

TOM: I much prefer to—to write it.

EVE: I know, Tom.

TOM: And most of the time— Well, most of the time—it works—

EVE: Yes.

TOM: But she—she—just doesn't fit— She's somehow—she's—too big— When I look at her—I can't— The words can't get hold of—the feelings—they won't do. They're not strong enough. *She's bigger than the words.* [*Realising, at last*] It frightens me.

    HENNY *moves towards* TOM.

HENNY: Of course it does.

TOM: I'm frightened, now. You've—do you see—you've started something—

HENNY *holds* TOM, *embraces him. He allows himself to be held like a child.*
HENNY: It's all right, really. It's quite all right. It's *better* than all right.
EVE: I see, now, what a fire might do. [*Beat.*] You and me—here together—pretending—pretending—while out there—out there—*things happen.* [*Beat.*] Is there anything stranger than locking your life into another's? Closing the door to the world and retreating, the two of you, into the depths of one another, the bizarre intimacy of that accord, agreeing to provide cover not for a weekend, or a vacation, but for all time?
TOM: [*realising too late*] I love belonging to you.
EVE: Lying side by side, dreaming there and then, in daylight, facing each other for another day of unquestioned company, banishing the night's spectacular journeys, their crazy betrayals and allegiances and summonings evaporated, and there we are, over the coffee pot... Sometimes I want to scream with fright that we are there again, again and again, in our dressing gowns pretending that it's normal and all we really want to say is: 'Who the Hell are You?' If that's not— grounds— If that's not—for seeking... *faith*... If that's not compelling as a means to something, something longer and larger than a lifetime, than ordinary heartbeats... I see now— Yes. Yes. What a fire might do.

Beat.

HARRY: [*to the audience*] It all started with a house. [*Beat.*] That's where it started. Sixty-two squares of timber and stone. Mansard roof, the loggia with wisteria, a return verandah and dry stone walls. Polished hardwood floors and fireplaces. Lights inlaid in the Italian-lavender-lined paths leading to the kitchen garden. French country kitchen with walk-in pantry. Parents' retreat complete with recessed lighting and wood panelling. No veneer. Nothing pokey. Just air and space and light. That's what it started with. A house.

Blackout.

THE END